Enough Light to See the Dark

FRANK DULLAGHAN

CinnamonPress

INDEPENDENT INNOVATIVE INTERNATIONAL

Published by Cinnamon Press
Meirion House, Glan yr afon, Tanygrisiau
Blaenau Ffestiniog, Gwynedd, LL41 3SU
www.cinnamonpress.com
The right of Frank Dullaghan to be identified as author of this
work has been asserted by him in accordance with the Copyright,
Designs and Patent Act, 1988. Copyright © 2011 Frank Dullaghan.
ISBN: 978-1-907090-90-5

British Library Cataloguing in Publication Data. A CIP record for
this book can be obtained from the British Library.

Designed and typeset in Palatino by Cinnamon Press.
Cover from original artwork by Aidan Dullaghan BA (Fine Arts) –
Enough Light to See the Dark, oil on canvas 102 cm x 81cm © Aidan
Dullaghan, used with kind permission.

Cover design by Jan Fortune

Printed in Poland

Cinnamon Press is represented in the UK by Inpress Ltd
www.inpressbooks.co.uk and in Wales by the Welsh Books
Council www.cllc.org.uk.

Acknowledgements

These poems, or earlier versions of them, have appeared in the following places: *Chirmea* (France); *Crannog* (Ireland); *The Dark Horse*; *Envoi*; *First Pressings* (Faber & Faber); *Glasgow Review*; *Ink, Sweat & Tears*; *The Honest Ulsterman*; *London Magazine*; *Magma*; *New Poetry Ventures website*; *Nimrod* (USA); *The North*; *Poetry Ireland Review*; *Reactions*; *Revival* (Ireland); *Seam: The Shop* (Ireland); *Smiths Knoll*; *Stand*; *Teaching a Chicken to Swim* (Seren Press); and *The Warwick Review*. A number of these poems were (as with my previous collection) work-shopped with Mo McAuley; Malcom Lewis; Sarah Salway; and Victor Tapner – my thanks guys for your input. Many of these poems were first performed at the Poeticians venue in Dubai – my thanks to Hind Shoufani for providing the platform. Thanks is also due to Ann Drysdale for her close reading of these poems and her invaluable assistance in putting the collection together. Thanks to my son, Aidan, for supplying the cover artwork. Finally, as always, thanks to my wife, Marie, for attending to most of these at their birth.

The haiku on the dedication page was published in my haiku collection *at the opened door* Hub Editions 2001.

Biography

Frank Dullaghan is an Irish poet, living and working in Dubai, UAE. He holds an MA with Distinction in Writing from Glamorgan University. Frank is a previous editor of *Seam* poetry journal and was one of the founders of the *Essex Poetry Festival*. He is a member of the Dubai performance poetry platform *Poeticians*, the *Emirates Literary Group* and the *Dubai Writers Group*. Frank has given poetry readings, run workshops and given seminars in Dubai and Sharjah and has read at the Emirates Literary Festival each year since 2009. His first poetry collection *On the Back of the Wind* was published by Cinnamon Press in 2008.

Contents

only myself
in the train window
these dark evenings

for Marie, Aidan, Fergus & Lynsey

Bride

after Frida Kahlo

Each evening now your pain goes out
and sits in a bar
with a drink the colour of the sun.

Your body has become a canvas.
You create yourself. Remember
how your red dress

would smoke about you.
Such delicate hurt. When your hair's loose
the moon seems to drown.

You step out like a bride.
So much blood,
petals of it scattered like confetti.

The stars are falling.
They have lost their sticky light.
They are accidents. They shed themselves.

And now
those babies you always wanted
call out in your sleep.

So we wait with our candles –
enough light to see the dark
when it comes.

October 1954

The gate would have closed without squealing
and the white pebble-dash may have, for a moment, turned

$$copper,$$

as the sun burned itself down behind fields
that had yet to be filled with houses.

I can see him standing, taking the pleasure of a last pipe.
A new end-of-terrace house. Working.

His first son curled to sleep in his cot. His wife in the doorway.
The life he had yet to make his way through

as clean as the fields. I would not have even entered his head
as he shrugged off the cold, tapped his pipe out

on the edge of the path and looked up
into the startlingly young face of my mother.

Starting Over

When mammy died he wanted to lid himself away,
realising too late he knew nothing
about household chores, rearing children.
We older ones left home, watched and judged.

Each night he sat stacking the coins
of his responsibilities, figuring
when the debt would be paid, reciting her name
when I came to visit, like a penitent's Hail Mary.

His hair turned white in months,
the house turned dark – an old man's house
with its stacked papers, its dusty pictures,
he wearing the same clothes until they stank.

I think he liked the idea of himself,
somehow heroic, struggling on alone
with two teenage sons, the blazing rows.
Out of his depth until I came to visit

with a baby he would take
crying from my arms, soothe in seconds,
cupping small feet in the warmth of his palm.
Then I remembered – he was always good at beginnings.

Batteries in Series and in Parallel

We were coming close to the end
of that time together, that weekly walk
half-way into town, then the mile road
to the railway station. I suppose
there were things he wanted to say.
I had exams going on, expectations
about the long possibilities of the world.

He was closed into his routine
of weekend fatherhood, work-away weeks.
He asked me how I was doing.
I had one exam left – General Science.
I only know about the theory of electricity,
he said, needing to give me something.
So we talked a slow mile of Ohms Law,

of batteries in series and in parallel.
He never understood that he's given me
more than the answer to a question
that turned up next morning but that he'd
told me all those things a father wants to say
if only the words would come,
if only the son knew how to listen.

The Quart Can

My father would send me down
to Fagen's with the quart can.
I'd bring it back brimming with dark porter
which he would slosh into his glass
where it browned, then darkened,
before he brought it to his lips and broke
the white wafer blessing the surface.

It was his Sunday evening sacramental
sin, slipped as he was from his usual unsociability,
though never as far as walking
to the pub himself, to its dark congregation,
its sticky altar. How long had I understood
that he had lost his surety, that heaven
was more of a guess than a promise?

I would watch him drink his dark glass
as the kitchen in our end-of-terrace home shrunk
and lost its gravity, I home from England
with my own family, the pull of the world
tall in me so that I knew enough
not to be a father to him, just a son
who'd rinse out his can, place it back on the shelf.

On the Coalhouse Roof

for Peter

I was away when the attack came,
your asthma suddenly brutal,
your heart climbing each moment

to take in a breath. The whole
of a morning, most of the afternoon.
How could our father just watch?

When we were small
a baby bird fell from the sky.
Its mother had been teaching it

to fly from a nest on our roof.
But it found no buoyancy in its wings,
its fright tightening them in, perhaps.

There it sat in the matted grass
crying as its mother circled.
Down she would swoop,

dive-bombing her baby, then up,
as if seeking some magnetic attraction
that might lift the young one

from the grass. Hours went by,
the mother sometimes only coming
as close as the coalhouse roof,

the baby losing its cry to exhaustion.
When the mother flew off, we went out,
you and I, and lifted its tiny fright

in our hands, one to the other.
You had the idea to put it
in a shallow box on the coalhouse roof.

I climbed the fence, eased it up.
All night long you watched
the ghost of that box in the dark.

I slept. In the morning we found it
dead in the yard. You had missed
its last leap into the night,

as I missed yours, your heart stumbling
and missing its steps, the doctor late,
un-chased, taking his time, our father
in his useless deference, waiting.

At the Gate

Even the blackest of rooks
cracking a yellow eye
at the dusk

or that syrupy cat
freezing its flow
through the border hedge,

do not distract him.
He lets night un-blaze
over the rooftops,

lets the solid soften,
the certainty of the
dimensional world shift.

He can feel portals open
the way tissues dissolve
in water, the way shapes

resolve out of fog.
This is how you will find him –
waiting at the gate

for that sharp instant
his father may choose
to come back to him.

What We Carry

I let you go, I did not count the cost
of losing or the burden you'd become.
We carry with us everything we've lost.

I thought we'd had our time, said all, but just
as I was moving on, here's your return.
What we let go is what we want the most.

So now I have this converse with your ghost,
that follows me, that's made itself at home.
We carry with us everything we've lost.

How can I exorcise you, I'm the host?
And anyway, I do not want you gone.
What we let go is what we want the most.

Perhaps there's more to say, another crust
to gnaw at in my head (that other tomb).
We carry with us everything we've lost.

Oh heart, be quiet, is this your double boast:
that you kept yourself otherwise engrossed;
that to let go is how we love the most?
We carry with us everything we've lost.

Castletown Bridge

It sat squat-heavy above the road,
low against the sky,
the road dipping under it

so that in heavy rain it flooded
and we schoolchildren would watch
for drivers new to the road

and its dip, who would plough
into the water, furrows of it
rising on either side then falling

as the car spluttered and stilled,
the driver sitting appalled
in the bridge's under-lake.

The footpath stayed on a level,
so we could look down
at the victim from our high railing.

But this was a rare occurrence.
Going home from school, though,
we could daily catch the Belfast train

as it thundered across. I learned
to brave the under-judder,
let noise take over, stand

on the edge of panic,
red flakes of rust raining down
through the sliced light.

Older boys would climb up, after,
and cross the trembling steel
to appear again, small gods

on the other side, a kind
of rite of passage until one boy
went over the top,

climbing early to stand
like an exclamation and scream
back at a screech of metal.

I held back after that, afraid
of the red swirl of rust,
of meeting his ghost.

The Heart's High Cliff

for Mary

I stand beyond a silent curve of cars
beside my sister,

leaves shine clean after rain,
the grass wet-jewelled about us,

she holds my arm.
Her boy lies in a box at our feet,

spun from the corner of a road,
his buckled bicycle,

flung from the heart's high cliff,
a breath's slim ledge.

Her weight suddenly on me
as they lower him down.

Her eyes as if some inner eyelid
shut.

Overcoat

I marvelled
at each new revelation –
the moonlight in her hair,
her nipple-puckered blouse.

I became the drunken owner
of touch, of lip
breaching lip, of the raw
startling delicacy

of the tip of a tongue.
We kept our own time,
burrowing into my army surplus coat
each evening after school.

And we got to know each shadow
on the road above the town,
whether hung between a gable
and a fence or where

a tree leaned upon a wall.
I became expert
at lip-reading her body
in the dark

and the envy of my peers,
who never knew how easy
it would be for her to go,
leaving half my coat empty.

St Patrick's Night

for John

By the time we reached that pub I was lost,
the city streets swaying at my back.

We squeezed ourselves in around a table
where spilt beer gleamed and the gloom

beyond the arc of the lamp seemed warm.
My brother eased another black glass

across into place – a priest of the night,
white collar glowing – I bowed my head

brought the pint up to my mouth,
the shamrock holding its shape on the froth

till I slurped. St. Patrick would have stood
in the cold, his beard floating,

his voice sending dark shapes slithering
through grass and clover, down gullies, over rock,

off into the sea, banished
from the hard shores of Ireland.

We are emigrants tonight, my brother and I,
gone beyond the shores of ourselves,

letting songs conjure us back
to a land just the same as this one

but held differently in our imagination,
our voices rising up to the high smoky ceiling,

out into the drizzle and the wind, as the longing
inside us uncurls and for a moment is gone.

Dundalk

This is the town that I left, its high-
ceilinged classrooms, the smell and weight
of a new year's school books,
the De La Salle brothers with their canes
beating learning into working class boys,
the wrought-iron gate to the train station,
a portal to elsewhere, the churches dark
with silences, that one hip northern priest with
his good looks, who came to the house
when my pregnant sister got married,
for the small after-meal my mother put out,
who refused to acknowledge the figure of shame
that padded about and sat between us
but belted out his voice in song to celebrate
the union, the coming child, and filled us
with the extraordinary knowledge
of ordinary things. This is the town where
my brother came home once broken
and bloody, where I first cupped the marvel
of a girl's breast, earned money, drank.
This is the town where I dreamed
of the possible in its many coats, though
never once dreamed myself dressed and away
from the accents and small certainties
of that parish. It is the town where my mother
finally let go of herself, where my brother's
heart gave out, where my father died slowly,
becoming more insubstantial with each sin
he acknowledged in himself. This is the town
that I left, a town where my sisters still live,
anchoring it to its past, as it grows a bright
new plumage and tries to fly away from me.

Waiting for Hooves

I was ten when they thundered
themselves large,
from the gypsy encampment,
freezing me in the headlights of their eyes
as the great engines of their bodies
crashed through their gears
and their manes spumed out behind them.
They steamed between
front garden walls and parked cars.
I froze on their track, watching them grow
into clamorous majesty;
froze till some other part of my brain
clicked in, leapt me aside
to watch their high heads
race down the line of the hedge
from the station of a neighbour's garden.

Tonight the river is a steel rail
beneath a gun-metal sky.
The drum of my skin tenses, waiting
for the next moment to slam into now,
for the hoof-hammer hit to catch the back of my eye
and explode down the rail,
gallop its iron through my head.
I want that rush of noise that I felt as a boy,
something to pick me up and fling me
from the worn path of myself
as the wind snorts and stamps
and the sky whinnies.

Two Poems for Marie

Losing the Language

You were good at the language,
not the English we spoke every day
but the older air of Irish,
fluent with the curl and ride
of its notes on your lips.
And I knew enough of it myself
to be easy in my listening.

Those first years in Birmingham
you would call me at work
from the headache of your desk,
your concerns wrapped in a melody
that could not be decoded
by your listening colleagues or boss.
And I knew enough of it still
to respond in a mongrel tongue.

Today the need to get by in the tough
aftermath of an economic crash
has me distanced in Dubai.
Now when you call, your English
lilts the line in an echo of that song.
But the Irish, you say, is lost:
infrequent use leaving you tone-dumb.
And I don't know enough anymore
even to hum.

Slowing the Bus

You got so big, the driver
would hold the bus,
stepping out to slow you
in your waddle-rush.

You worked until a week
before the birth.
Standing sideways, you filled
our bedroom door.

When going to the loo,
you had to sit down first
then kick the door closed,
stand up again to lock it.

I'd never seen you happier
than with that weight.
This was something you knew
you would do well.
You were swell.

Rabbit

for Aidan

I was walking with my tall son,
both of us hunched into our jackets,
our hands deep in our pockets,
heads down against the wind.
There was a bond of hurt between us.

We were heading for an appointment
he had with his psychiatrist.
He was ill in those days,
thinking he was a rabbit.
We walked in silence.

We passed shop-front after shop-front,
their lights blaring onto the street.
There was a shape in a doorway
huddled on a cardboard bed,
blue face fuzzed with adolescent hair.

Poor bastard, I said, *did you see him?*
I turned my head to where
my son should have been.
I found him sharing space on the cardboard,
hung around trying not to look awkward.

When he rejoined me he said,
You know I'm the only rabbit
he's talked to in three days.
We walked on together as before,
letting the silence settle on our skins.

Weathering

We've re-pegged the sky to give more headroom.
Now the storm's gone that brought it flapping down
we can breathe more widely for a while,
as if there are no edges to the air.

We watch the day light to his careless smile,
want to believe he never was away,
getting lost in the dark howl of his head.
The doctor said he'd make it. But we watched

him break asunder and the sky rip loose.
We have no notion how we put it back
when it seemed its weathered weight would tip all
of us beyond the world we'd married.

But we seemed to find a way by accident
or fear. Now he moves about with that same odd grace
that my sister's three-legged cat wore,
dipping its shoulder as if bowing at her door

Orange

I want to unhinge him from his strangeness,
I want the perfect swish of the basketball through the net,
the fully controlled round-house kick
to the head, his boyish smile.

He goes off on long journeys of the mind
without a compass,
comes back terrified. He loses me.
I need a map of his head.

The doctor's prescribed medication, blood tests, scans.
It is late evening, London.
We watch traffic through the window
of a café on Regent Street.

Each car brightens the road as it passes.
I play with the orange in my coat pocket,
take it out to admire the gleam of its skin, its roundness.
Perfect, he says. *Whole.*

Named

Delusional: the paranoid flinch of the eye
when the eye feels held; the creak and swivel of cameras
on their high mounts, watching.
His own horror movie.
His friends eyes searing him. Everyone.
So that all he can do is lope off, crouched under the furrow
of his brow, go to ground in some dark space
between two walls; in some corner.

The doctor has put a name on it,
tentatively, as if the gum on the label might not hold.
Looking across at our son, we know him better.
Outside, rain has returned,
its patter and dance soft on the window.
My son's voice finds its feet,
steadies, in the to and fro of our talk.
More tests. To be sure. A program
like a journey that will bring him back.

But named! Now he'll have power over it.
Now we can conjure a recovery.
Temporal lobe epilepsy.
The doctor rises like a priest
to bless us, shake our hands,
agree the next appointment for our son.
The opened door fills with sky.

Until Morning Comes

Sky has entered water.
What is below is now the same
as what is above.

After the ocean drank down the sun,
night grew cold.

There was blood on the surface,
as if there had been a great slaughter.
But there had been no struggle.
Sea opened its purse
and the sun slipped in.

My son will not speak of the moon.
It is a great ear in the sky.
He will keep his voice secret.

How many windows, he wonders,
has the human body?
In particular,
how many for looking in?
He needs to be careful.

In the dark, water takes to the air,
opening out its wet wings
it lifts its great body high
and feasts on the stars.

Nothing is ever what it seems.
Wind moves through.
But it will not stay.

This is how it always is –
the dark making him a stranger.
Even his face may have fled.

Until morning comes,
it may never come.

Atlantic

Kenmare, Co Kerry, Ireland

We stand beside Atlantic rage.
Rain hammers into rock,
the strand a sleek of wet.
Sky has drowned. Air calls out
to the old gods.

There are no words
we can mouth, it will not swallow.
The cliff behind us
has lost its hold on the world.
It will never be solid again.

Your hair flings itself about you.
Your skirt rips at your legs.
My eyes swim, my head,
a kettle holding thunder.
All is purple-blue, all

plunges into charcoal, rush and wind.
I am trying to hold,
each atom linking arms with the next,
their small fists clenched hard
over their hearts,

their nails anchored
into the flesh of their palms.
But it's not enough.
I need to find an edge to grab onto,
some small roughness,

even an abrasion of air,
that will slow this shifting away.
Now the sound of your voice
lifts my face, turns it wet
on this our last day of grace.

Playing With Water

The tattered tongue of the rising tide
licks at your feet. The broken sea
drags the horizon closer.
A day moon ghosts the sky,
hanging there bereft of luminance
like something fallen out of love.

The sun sheds itself,
its molten leaves blinding the water.
You shade your eyes.
You know it is all an illusion.
The water is a weight of dark
heaving its body between two coasts,

gnawing its way closer,
its cold heart hammering away
under its sparkling skin.
It tries to tease you with its silk
ruffs, its glimmer. But if you lie down here
it will rise up and devour you.

It has no word for hunger
that is not the name
that it calls itself. The day crumbles
before it, gulls comb its hair,
the strand winces under its touch.
And always that rumble in its belly

as it tries to lure you in.
Still you walk this line of sand
staring at it, as if you have some alchemy
to tame it, some circle of protection
that might save you from its passion
should it decide to storm in and claim you.

You hold the thought of water in your head
but it will not be contained.

The Creosote Jar

She kept a creosote jar under her bed,
stolen from a batch her father had
to keep the fence from rotting in the wet
of Irish winters. She liked its smell,

that gold-brown bloom of pungent mystery.
She inhaled it every night.
We were both seventeen and testing
the masteries of life – how touch

can bind; the power that rests in certain
words; the way the dark could wrap us
in ourselves. She offered me the jar
like it were a holy thing, a sacrament.

I took it in a slow half-hearted way,
afraid to spill it but knowing then, too late,
her need to feel that edge of danger
that I did not quite have.

Gluttony

I loved to watch her sitting
where that park tree
spread its cool on the grass,
where my mind got a notion of wine
from the tilt of her mouth.

But taste like that was dangerous.
I could fall so far into it –
its subtle addiction,
its smooth easy ways and its rough.

Yet how could I give her up –
that need to gorge on her laugh,
her hip flaring out
to my gluttonous touch?

She was there on the tip
of my tongue. I was head over heels
in the taste of her skin.
There was never enough.

But enough was enough
when she left me,
for I could not shut it off –
the light forever lifting up her shape
from the sun-yellowed grass.

Telling Stories

for Marie

You invited a teaching colleague and her husband over.
We were young, learning to entertain.
We didn't know them well. I had my instructions:
when to pour the wine; not to hog the conversation.

After dinner, we left the cooling coffee cups, the plate
of untouched chocolate mints. I loosened myself
into a sofa chair, a second bottle of red darkening
in our glasses. They took a formal pose on the settee,

knees together, hands in laps. I suppose they were learning too.
He may have had his own instructions. But you
were softened by the wine and went with habit,
sitting on the floor between my legs, head on my knee.

We drank and told stories. Trying to coax some informality,
some touch-point with them, we bantered with each other.
We were highly physical in those days, spending
our time together on judo mats or in karate halls.

So I expressed my disagreement with something you said
by sliding a friendly choke around your throat.
You countered not by breaking it, as I expected (it was
loosely on), but by reaching back and grabbing me,

where I'd brought my head softly to your shoulder, and
rising slightly, pitching me out of the chair.
Going over, even in the laze of wine, I knew your move
was technically superb and not to be outdone (in front of guests)

I twisted in mid-air to hook a leg, then swivelled to apply
an arm-lock, gain submission. We were high in the delirium
of our entanglement before we registered our guests,
heels up on the settee, faces blanched. We did explain

what normal was for us; that we were trained; this sport.
But they remembered that their babysitter couldn't stay too late.
It is agreed, we finished up the wine, the chocolate mints,
but not whose fault it was nor who had won.

Imagination

for Thomas

The night after my mother died
my brother, who was nine, stopped crying.

He told us she had come to him,
sat on the edge of his bed

in the half-dark of the back bedroom.
It's all right, was what he said she said.

He'd always had a vivid imagination,
believed in his own tales.

I woke, he said, *with the weight of her
on the bed. She was real,*

I couldn't see through her.
Only the mind can go beyond

its own sepulchre, its own white bone.
So much have we plundered there

and made real –
voices from half a world away;

memory you can carry in your pocket.
So Thomas brought my mother back,

having the mind to do it.

Sailor

for Rosemarie

You sunk your well
where the hazel dipped.
Water rose sure and clean,
coming up to you
from the cold folds of the hill.

Now standing in the whip-wind
off the gable, gazing across
a grey lap of fields,
it seems as if this place
floats through the evening.

Braced wide-legged
against the roll of the ground,
I look towards the house,
your head bowed in the window.
And I could be a sailor

within sight of land,
waiting for the tide to turn,
as your face lifts up
and your hand
beckons me in.

My MG Maestro

In the end it was too much. But back then
when it was new, and smelt new, I showed it off
to everyone, inviting them into the front
passenger seat, starting off without clicking
so it would say *Please fasten your seat belt*
in its posh female voice. My father said *Sorry*
the first time though he'd already belted himself in.
But then it said *Oil low* and *Mileage high*,

The morning is a blue balloon and *I am
a magpie*. It said, *The Mothership is coming* and
Everything starts with zero. In the end no one
would travel with me. In the end it sat on my drive
reciting ten-word love poems to itself .
In the end they came for it and I let it go.

Knowledge

She's such a strange little girl,
telling me she's afraid her eyes will fall out.

She walks around with her hands over her face,
a drunk bumping the walls. A walking terror.

At night she moans. *How will I know?* she asks me,
If I lose one, it will just be gone.

Have you ever known anyone whose eye has fallen out? I ask.
She lists her dolls, her dreams, a cartoon character.

The walls are bending away from me. *A person?* I say.
I could be the first, she whispers, *you never know.*

An Only Child

It was a ghost on her shoulder,
a feeling of carrying more than herself,
an unseen wing folded back into her.

She'd been told the story, of course,
of the twin who never made it out,
dying in her mother's womb,

shrivelling back into the placenta,
a *foetus papyrus*. As a child
it doubled as her guardian angel.

And now? Just there, her *alter ego*,
an identical spirit whose physical absence
she wears like a charm.

The Short Cut

for Steve

Never one for the straight road,
you took us through snow-tucked fields
on a *short-cut* to the village that always
took longer, as the sun stretched over the hedges
and the sky opened white.

It was past mid-day when we eventually
found our way onto streets,
bright from heavy-footing lost ways,
the clean fields etched with our tracks.

Later, in the slow hour before sleep,
we drank and spoke of the span
of our lives, the way time never stops.
And you glanced sharply about
as if seeking some twist or loop

that would let you double back
on yourself, search out a *short-cut*,
come late to the end, your map of footprints
well stamped on the landscape.

Flying in a Pink Leotard

Mid-Nineties, Broadgate Arena, London,
when the sky could hardly limit,
I took a lunchtime stroll
to daydream riches.

It was easy then, the future
always another floor up.
There in the sun-rich square,
a trapeze had been erected and a girl

in a pink leotard risked the open air,
trusting her skill against a free-fall,
the arc of her body rising
in the mirrored windows of investment banks.

She was a sure creature of heaven,
as if she would never
have to touch down,
take the underground home from the city.

Halloween

We are coming into that time
when things are not fully themselves –
sky improperly dresses in glint and shadow,
buildings slant from the vertical,
birds toss themselves from bare branch to branch.
Even the voice slips from the mouth
without its coat.
                              My mother
(remembered here from that photograph)
pegs a sheet to a line, the pebble-dashed wall
of the shed catching and breaking
the white light of morning behind her,
her mouth open but silent, her eyes
trying to hold what is already leaving.
Days not fully themselves.
                              Neither now nor then.
When do we ever close the face of the past,
lay copper suns on its eyelids,
bind its bony fingers with rosary beads?
Nothing dies completely. On nights
like this even death
finds it hard to retain its certainty.

In the Country of the Dark

Sit, watch, wait for the *Fetch*
or some other member of the *Sidhe*
who dart and whip through the night dark,
conspire under the hooded moon,
gather near rowan or hawthorn,
make themselves manic with mischief.
Masters of wind-knocked windows,
a blocked flue's stutter,
the tap-tap at the empty door.

Sit and be quiet, for you dare not go out
where the *Fear Dearg* or the *Pooka*
pass the wink to each other
that you are out of your element,
where fear might gather you up,
blow you blind into the black,
far beyond your own front door.

Daddy's Little Girl

You would have been Daddy's little girl
if there'd been an elder son
to hoist his name's flag. What he got
was the shame of four daughters.

You would have been if it wasn't
for that streak of viciousness he wore,
his bullet-proof vest in a world gunning for him,
and you there, a spare target,

so self-righteous, taking a son's share
of good school reports, boy's sports.
You would have been his little girl
in your frock, your blaze of red hair,

if you'd kept your mouth shut,
if you'd learned to put up, if you'd not
found fault with the turn of your head,
with that look, if you'd been someone else,

some other place. You'd have been
Daddy's girl if you'd used your imagination
and didn't need a hug, need proof.
Your sights were set too high by half,

the fatted calf, wanting everything right.
Wasn't he the man of the house, a house
that he'd built? It was he who put the food
in your mouth, the stick on your back.

Fairy Tales

In your telling of it, that farm cottage
held all the detailed charm
of a painting – the sun purring
against its white walls, its half-door
opening onto a yard of hens, and
a tractor standing noble in its red coat.

But touch the paint and it will flake
to half-truths and closed spaces,
to bog-dark silences and pain
tight as a body bag. It has more to do
with rough hands and a young girl's
sudden knowing than playful lambs.

This is the dark within the fairy tale,
the old story dressed up for the neighbours.

Room

You sit with your mother,
not pushing her to eat or take tablets
but letting her cry, letting her go back
through the rooms of her life,
letting her tell you what she held
locked in the house of her head since a girl,
a time when an open door was a trap,
when the chink of a smile
could let the dark through.

The road outside is drowned in night.
Everyone tells her to rest, she says.
They don't want to know she's afraid.
You say that you read somewhere
that a baby's heartbeat panics
just before birth, the baby wanting to stay
in the pulse of the womb.
light from a passing car scans the stains on the wall.
The room shrinks back to her voice.

Time

for Marie

Your plane is down. Dark has lifted back into the sky.
I watch people spill through the arrivals door
like pebbles from a pouch tipped-up,
search for your face, the colour of your coat.
Home from home. Your mother, in a hospital ward in Dublin,
is wearing out her day, finding that it fits
too loosely on her bones – a frayed, thread-bare dress,
hardly enough to hold her breath within.

Almost an hour's wait. Time at its tricks,
freeze-framing me against my wristed watch
whilst back in Ireland, your mother finds her day
fast-forwards, as they all do now, so she is forever going
to sleep. Now here you come, opening your arms.
Soon enough we will all reach that place
where time cracks open, lets go of us.
Come here. There'll be no time then for ourselves.

The Long Sleep of Dragons

The dragons are growing old.
They darken and harden
into their concrete skins,
their scales yellow with lichen.

They are perched on the battlements
of ancient churches. They watch
with red eyes for a second coming.
Only at night, occasionally,

might one un-crank its wings
and cast a deeper shadow on the dark
gliding out over rooftops, parks.
Sleepers stir feeling it pass

like an eclipse of the soul.
The clack of its ebony flight
causes trees to tremble
into their held blackness

and the blacksmith, working late,
to whiten his iron.
They have no more desire for gold
or the hoarding of stone.

They have lost faith
with what the world has become.
They refuse to confirm us
with their fiery majesty.

Crossing

It was some years ago.
The fields had tucked
themselves in for the night
and the sky could hardly
keep its eye open.

There were no markers,
the grey of one holding
spilled into the next.
The high hedges pushed
the road over the hills.

Light cracked a corner.
On the straight
a man waved a lamp, a gun
black in his other hand.
The road stopped

to slow shadows,
balaclavas, eyes,
unblinking muzzles.
At the lowered window
a mouth smoked words,

ordinary words
familiar to an ear
at any border crossing –
Where are you travelling?
Where have you come from?

But here, out of nowhere;
out of the flat slap
of trees against windscreen;
the settled hum of the mind:
terror.

Not that anything happened –
the licence taken,
noted as British;
my accent – *Border boy,*
home on holidays, are you?

It was the way the quiet
wrapped about us;
his clean blue eyes;
the slowness of his hand
returning my papers.

Emer's Sister Mourns the Death
of Cuchulainn

You had it coming and you knew it.
Emer looked stunning in black,
the perfect widow,
full of her keening.
She never cared that much.
You were never at home –
off with your gun;
your bloody Red Branch Knights,
always over the border.

They found you tied to a stone,
slouched in the sticky tar
of your blood, a raven,
black as your soul,
on your shoulder.
They filled the streets,
out from their small houses
to watch your black chariot pass;
your wife a prune of grief;
the hard men getting ready to spill
your glory out in the corner bars.

Now its Emer this and Emer that.
Television. Newspapers. Her pretty face
burning from every wall. Euro MP.
No time for her older sister.
Never a mention, not even my name.

But I was there when it started,
when you came courtin'
with your smirks and your riddles,
your dangerous beautiful body.

58

I was the one they all said (you?) would marry,
not her, sitting with her needles
and her virgin's blush.
I would have been good for you.
I know how to keep a man at home.

Unsaddled

I was thinking of Oisin
on his careless holiday from the Land of Youth
(how happy and young he'd felt there)
and of his lover waiting for him
with her eyes and her soft limbs.

When leaning from his horse to help
(his generosity overcoming him)
frail men move a mighty rock,
he should have known
his luck would not hold out.

The girdle of his saddle burst
and he was pitched to earth,
the ordinary muck of life,
(how easily you can return to it!)
with no way back; no second chance.

He stood up, bent and shocked
in that gawking world of men
(this is no fantasy, this is pain)
and he grew old and silent
in that moment's blinking eye.

I wonder if his lover in that other place
(now a struggled image in his head;
now almost make-believe)
turned her face away
all cold and stern.

Lament for My Sea Maiden

The world is white.
The sun cowers behind a white sky.
Ice has captured all sparkle.
The sea lies like a dead sailor,
its grey blanket over its head.
The wind sharpens its knife.

Yet I stand looking out,
searching for the green gleam of your skin,
fooling myself it could all be the same –
the window burned against the snow,
the door dark in its frame,
you surging over me in bed,

all breaker and wave-crash.
I, who stole you from the waves,
saw you scald yourself again
in a moon-flecked sea, escapee
calling to me, wanting me deep
in your hunger; I who watched

you slice like a seal
through black water, stand now
in a white flurry. I would freeze
the dark blood-ache in my bones.
Call me. Call me again.
I will come.

Mastery

Seamus Heaney & Liam O'Flynn - Barbican Hall 28/3/99

Here, during the break in the poetry
reading at the Barbican, we all line
up with our heads bowed, an asymmetry
of gold glitter splashed on white porcelain,
and no one talking but breathing softly,
released, and now at ease in the after-
time of poet and piper's mastery,
holding our own counsel. Sounds of water

in the basins behind us feel homely
and of a one, too, with the occasion –
making a wonder out of ordinary
words; notes blown through a reed, and a notion
of how the extraordinary's just part
of our own selves, if we knew where to start.

Meeting the Man

I leave my car in the heat,
the sand-coloured sky an open oven,
and walk in my blue suit.
I walk down the length
of this make-shift car park,
walk around the fencing and building works,
walk the wobbling boards laid down
on the sand, here in Dubai
where all building works now move
like the ruminative old.

Inside the CID Headquarters, it is cool –
a long crowded counter, a waiting area,
a policeman in a green uniform
by an inner door, a black holstered gun.
I have come to meet the senior man
at his request, one whose name
gains quick response
so that I am let through into the compound
behind this building and directed
to another, an inner sanctum.

He is the head of the secret police,
I was told. *He has more faces than you'd guess.*
I meet him in a small untidy office.
He's a man at ease with himself.
Sure. Educated. *I'm just back from Ireland,*
he says when he hears my accent,
sweeping his white gutrah behind his shoulder,
tidying the sleeve of his crisp dishdash,
and getting down to business.

Gutrah – scarf like head covering
Dishdash – white body dress

Where Will You Take Me

Afghanistan – Prosthetic Limb Desert Camp

I cover my head, my face.
Since you have taken back my name I am called:
Woman who is learning to walk.

Your eyes are as blue as the sky, you once said.
But blue will not stay blue
just as the eye turns away from the eye.

Here is your hand – it is folded away.
Here is your tongue – it is tied to its silence.
Here is your woman – I am no longer your woman.

Will you not walk with me,
place your feet beside my feet
which are not my feet?

Not every crippled woman is a crippled woman.
Where will you take me
if I show you my face?

I have come to this camp of cripples
to learn how to walk. Where
is the camp of the dumb?

I have painted my nails the colour of sin.
I wear make-up under my burka.
Where will you take me if I show you my nails?

Everything is at war –
even one grain of sand against another.
Why do you carry this bomb in your heart?

Am I a bad woman?
Where will you take me
if I show you my legs?

The Soldier

I was down by the river when the soldier came.
He laid his gun on the ground and knelt to drink.

I became bush, rock, soil, became invisible. Still he saw me
and came, grinning like a wolf,

wiping his hands down his thighs, sweating.
His rifle was careless in his hand. Its dark steel

caught a shine from the river. *Ah, a little girl*, he said.
My feet were cold stone, my heart was pelting rain .

He lifted the hem of my skirt with his gun barrel.
I could smell him, all heat and sweat. I held myself still,

the way I saw a frog do once, when cornered by a dog.
He licked his lips. I closed my eyes to make him disappear

and prayed to Allah to take the moment from me.
Then his comrades came and laughed, took him away.

When I made it home my mother was wailing.
The soldiers had blackened the village, smoke hung

like a flag from our gable. I never
told her. But that night I could still feel it –

the cold hard prod of his gun on my belly,
the shiver at what might have happened.

In a Place of Darkness

Sia-sarah the man called us, *Black-heads,*
because of our black hijabs.
He demanded to know
where our fathers were, our brothers.

He would have beaten us, being unaccompanied,
had Waheed not come and looked at him,
the way a hawk might look at a mouse,
a stallion at a whelp of a dog.

I took my husband home and washed his hair.
Though there was no glass left
in our window, that night the curtains
held the cold to the street.

*

I would meet Laila by the stream
under the pomegranate trees.
We would splash our faces and talk of her trouble.
Not another day with him, she would say.

When she went to the courts for a divorce
I wanted to stay at home, admire the broad back
of my own husband, a sail rising from the sea
of our bed. I wanted to float there with him forever.

But I had him take me. *It's a man's court,* he warned,
she will win nothing but another beating.
Laila was silent when they told her
to go home and be obedient to her snarl of a husband.

The colour was sudden, the blue aura of it, the flash
into gold, red; into shrieking, writhing, black; into hands
of flame, a voice no longer hers hammering
at Allah's door. And all the men were silent.

*

When war came everything I knew was flattened.
First my voice,
then the light in my head.

Now there is just day, then night.
They just happen
the way smoke and blood happen.

And noise.
Sometimes it's another's noise,
though mostly it's my own.

When war came,
it came all the way inside
and then nothing was quiet ever again.

*

The birds are fighting.
They stab and slash at each other.

They have razors in their beaks.
They go for an eye, a throat.

Pain is what they feed on now –
a broken wing, a ruptured breast.

They have no interest in the sky,
only this feast of death and dying.

*

I take my blue shawl from the chest
just to have colour in the room.
Sky blue Waheed said when he bought it for me.
But the sky has been rotted with smoke and dust.
Everything is black, even the blood
burnt into the street.

Waheed used to say *Allah makes all things beautiful.*
If you look, you see. But Waheed is gone,
a shadow running through the hills.
I am nothing now.
I am just a woman holding on
to a blue shawl in the dark.

*

There are many shades of black.
There's the black that comes at night,
its faceless voice banging out of the dark.
There's the morning black when the day
heaves the great hump of its back
in front of the sun. There's the black of the heart,
its black river flowing inside me.
Then the black I have seen within the flame.
And, in shame, the black of my mouth cursing Allah.

Look at that bird in its black tree.
It could easily fly from this place of darkness.
Yet still it remains pecking at its black deeds.
If it were to go, it would carry
its own small blackness with it.
I am like that bird, my soul black within me.
I would come into the new with the stain of the old.
The man called us *Sia-sarah* because of our black hearts.

The Trial and Abjuration of Joan of Arc

1

I am Joan, daughter of Jacques d'Arc.
I was born in 1412. I am Nineteen years old.
I broke the English siege at Orleans.
At Rheims I crowned the Dauphin king.

The first time I heard the voice, I was very frightened.
It was midday, summer, the sky was lazy.
I was at the bottom of my father's garden.
Even the bees were asleep.
When I heard it again, I knew
it was the voice of an angel. It was beautiful,
soft and humble. It gathered the brightness.
I told it I was a poor girl, knew nothing
of wars or royalty.
Go, daughter of God, it said. And I did.

2

Are you in God's grace?
For these churchmen everything is black and white –
as black as their holy robes,
as white as their washed feet.
They are full with learning, the knowledge
of right and wrong.
All I have is the truth.
If I am not, may God bring me to it.
If I am, may he keep me in it.

3

My voices had grown slow.
I rode for Paris because my men needed to,
not because I was bid to by God.
It was the way a ploughboy will speed up
the oxen team, believing
he has the straight line sure and so spoil the field.
I gave myself to my enemy.

4

Sometimes they leave the door open
so I will know the limits of my chains.
I fear that Death will step inside, bark
its cold bark at me.
I long for air and light.
But these are held prisoner outside
and only a small portion escapes
into my cell.

5

Why are men of power so sure?
These old men fear my youth.
They would make a bonfire of my maidenhood,
that I usurp their role, am close to God.
They tell me I will burn.
But what will they do for light when I go out?

6

Listen, the peal of the bells is free
on the wind. It is Easter-time.
I would ring my body like a bell.
I would be resurrected from this terror.
All of the rooms where they have taken me are small
except the room in my head.

7

They say that this country needs a torch
to chase the shadows back into their walls.
What I need is the sun,
to know that the bees sleep still,
and all the fighting done.

8

The Lord Bishop of Beauvais is stern.
His pink robe is sharp and fine.
It sits on him like a holy prayer that cannot be argued with.
He smells of soap.

They write down all that I say
but listen to nothing. He has already decided
my sentence in his heart.
You will be abjured, he says
and they take me out.
I smell the earth, the open air, and shiver.
They take me to a scaffold they've set up in the cemetery
to be preached in front of the people.
Death pads beside me.

The priest spits his prayers at me.
He exhorts me to recant, to be subject to the church,
knowing I will not.

The crowd grows restless,
wanting to see my flesh melt. *Burn
the witch*, they cry.
Death wags its tail, puts its cold nose on my belly.
Recant, the priest screams, looking at the crowd.

I see his tongue dart between his teeth
as if trying to escape.
I shake. My bones are sick.
My body is so noisy with fear.
I am lost. My eyes go back
to a red kerchief that flickers round the neck
of some woman in the crowd.
My flesh screams
for any comfort. Sobbing racks me.
Fear is my new lord.

The bishop has started into the long chant
of my sentence –
*sedition, idolatry, pride, claiming to come from God,
indecency, letting herself be received like a saint,
offering her armour as a relic, casting spells* –
His terrors blaze.

I hear myself shout a denial of my voices.
I promise to submit
to Holy Mother Church, to cast off men's clothes.
I make my mark on their page.

9

They do not send me, as they should,
to the church's prison, but give me to the soldiers.
I am chained to a bed in a cell.
They loosen my shirt, tug at my hose,
keep touching me, laughing their foreign laughs.
They take off their belts, take turns to pain me.
My cries are caged birds battering their wings on the bars.

10

The priests send me women's clothes.
The soldiers watch like wolves as I change.
The sergeant rams me back against the wall,
fumbles in his breeches, yanks up my skirts.
I feel the scald of him against my thigh.
Go to God, my voices say.

Then they bring my men's clothes back,
toss them on the floor, a black heap,
and unchain my body.
I dress. Maybe now God will find me again.
But the clerics come. They charge me
with relapse. *God where are you*
when I need to be full,
when I need your voice to cover my own.
A relapsed heretic will burn.

11

I remember my father,
the dark shape of him in a doorway,
his voice a crackling log, taking me up in his arms.

12

The people wear their hunger like teeth. It is strange
the way I can see so much,
chained like this above the crowd.
A murmur melts. They watch me silently
like I'm a fowl being prepared for a meal.
The executioner trembles tying my hands.
He keeps his eyes turned away.
There's a nick on his neck that bleeds.

13

My heart is a battleaxe which I lift again and again.
It is wearing me down. Death snarls.
Oh God, forgive my fear.
There is a whoosh of flame and the crowd flickers.
Death bares its teeth,
its growl is filled with the crowd's excitement.
Air incinerates. I breathe in fire.
It clings to me. Death mounts me. I am raw.
My skin tightens on my face.
My body is a howl. My mind wants to run.
A tail of smoke whips up. It stings.
They lift a cross to my face.
I scream for Jesus
(my cry toppling from my mouth
to fall between the paws of Death)
and He comes.

Ruin

i

I can see now how he came to this ruin
of himself. That wind-whipped, wind-

wiped, scattering of what he surely once
hoped would be greatness, was just a bunch

of stuff strung together by association.
It had no real worth, no structure. That notion

perhaps of a castle, a keep, something grand
and spiritual, in that wave-of-the-wand-

world that the church inhabited, that catholic
version of life – obedience and miracle – he let cut

into his heart, where it left its rough-scabbed mark
that he'd never measured up, not in his work,

not in his daily endeavour, not in physique,
but had slipped lazily (or speedily, looking back)

into the broken man he became: age-crocked,
cragged, clouded, lost in doubt, locked-

in, fogged, crumbled, tottered, claimed
by regret, and surely, surely cruelly, damned.

ii

Here are the four walls of myself.
These are the words that I raise as a roof.

Let the rain come, I've been weathered before.
These are my feet. My feet are my floor.

There is no need to knock. You can enter,
the door isn't locked. I am not my father.

The Record Player

for Marie

We brought the record player home
like it was a great prize. I had never owned one
and music in our small bed-sit
was a repeated miracle all that summer.
Everything shone. The future was more possible
than the past. Breathless. I was a pot bubbling over.
Do you remember?

Just out of Uni, working, money so new
and exciting. The things you could do with it.
If you pared it down and saved the shavings,
the things you could turn it into.

Do you remember the way we talked,
the way each moment was bright
when we turned them over, the discoveries we made?
Walking down those steps between high fences
to come, at a corner, on open water
stretching its dazzle at the edge of the city,
hidden behind houses. Wasn't that how it was?

I see you stopped in the doorway
of our home in Dubai, after I've hunted out
one of those old tunes, and watch it take you
by surprise, your face young with delight.

And isn't that how it should be for us now –
grand and easy, easy and grand?